Learning Pieces

by

Howard Stein

with a foreword by
Dr. Warren Lee Holleman

DORRANCE PUBLISHING CO., INC.
PITTSBURGH, PENNSYLVANIA 15222

ISBN # 0-8059-4786-8
Library of Congress Catalog Card Number: 99-093484
Printed in the United States of America

First Printing

For information or to order additional books, please write:
Dorrance Publishing Co., Inc.
643 Smithfield Street
Pittsburgh, PA 15222
U.S.A.
1-800-788-7654

Dedication

*Dedicated to G. Gayle Stephens, M.D.,
in friendship.*

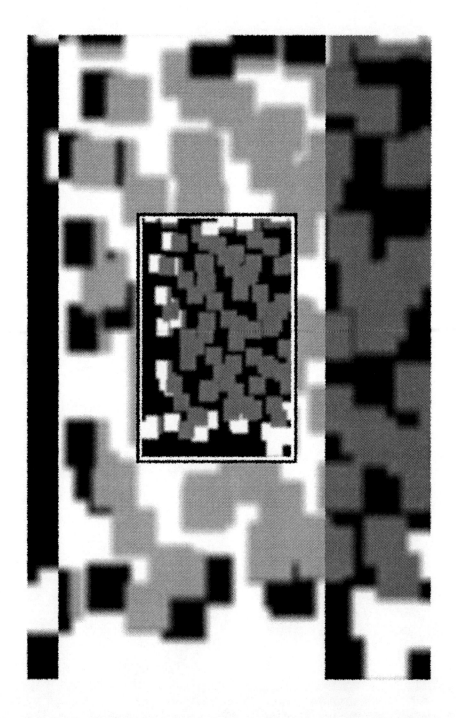

Contents

Foreword

Warren Lee Holleman, Ph.D.
"Art in Medicine" Editor,
The Journal of Family Practice

I first became acquainted with Howard Stein a few years ago when editing a textbook for medical students. We assigned Howard the chapter on "The Cultural World of the Patient" and expected a politically correct discourse on the health beliefs and practices of the standard "ethnic groups": African Americans, Hispanics, Native Americans, and so on. In the course of the chapter Howard did provide valuable information about such groups, but what permeated and distinguished the chapter was Howard's focus on a subculture not generally included in civil rights debates and diversity training workshops: the Midwestern American farmer. In a discussion of "noncompliance" for example, Howard presented the case of a seriously ill middle-aged patient who frightened and frustrated his physician by skipping an important appointment. The patient, it turned out, was a member of an ethnic group that placed a strong economic, moral, and religious value on getting the harvest in on time, and since the illness occurred during harvest season, the white Midwestern farmer quite predictably acted according to his value system. Since the doctor's belief system placed human health above all other values, and since the doctor did not understand or respect his patient's belief system, the doctor wrongly accused the patient of being unreliable and unfaithful to his commitments. Actually, the patient had been very faithful—to his land.

After editing Howard's chapter I was disabused of any notion that white people or any subgroup of whites were the "standard" and everyone else "diverse." I learned about my own prejudices in presuming that the purpose of such a chapter should be to sensitize white middle-class medical students to the values of non-white patients. Howard reminded me of the peculiarities and similarities of every subculture, including my own, and challenged me to stop viewing people like me as being at the center and those unlike me as being on the periphery. *My center of the earth / Has no angel's face. / It has spawned no special race, / Has no periphery beyond the reach / Of human grace. / It is neither more nor less / Than any other place.*

I first met Howard face-to-face at a breakfast discussion group of the annual meeting of the Society of Teachers of Family Medicine. The conversation that morning focused on how to train medical students and residents to treat indigent patients with compassion and respect. We talked our way around the table, sharing information; describing experiences; and offering insights, perspectives, and interpretations. We were well into the discussion when Howard joined us from another table. Howard listened attentively and, if this be possible, energetically. A noticeable shift occurred. People started trying harder to understand each other and to be more honest with their feelings. After taking it all in Howard spoke, more quietly than he had listened, and the conversation moved to yet another level. Instead of offering more information, more experiences, or more interpretations of this data, Howard offered observations and interpretations of the dynamics of our own conversation, pointing out that in our way of framing the conversation we ran the risk of viewing our students with the same cynicism and paternalism that we accused them of having toward their patients. As with the book chapter, Howard challenged us to reconsider the meaning and locations of *us* and *them*. I was amazed at how quickly and decisively he turned the conversation, yet appeared so unobtrusive and modest in the process as though *we* had given *him* the idea. *How clever you were / To rehearse us so well / In so unsuspecting a disguise: / How thoughtful a deception / To make a going seem / Almost like a return.* Or to make a criticism sound like a compliment or to make *his* idea appear to have evolved so naturally from *our* group process.

Once the conversation opened up to this level I recognized how placing myself self-righteously on the side of the solution meant that in some respects I was part of the problem. I began wondering what it would take to create spaces where doctors and patients and students and teachers *had no need for words / To parse a person by.* I also realized that I felt jealous and threatened by these students. *Where I am is where and who / You wish to be—to expand, to sprawl, / Into the office skin of me. . . . Space is parable / for both our dying.* Howard gets you to thinking about some serious stuff.

I became acquainted with Howard Stein the poet through reviewing poems he submitted to the *Journal of Family Practice*, where I serve as section editor of "The Art of Medicine" feature. Other writers usually send me poems and stories about their patients, their difficult cases, their feelings about their work. Howard was different. He sent me poems about the prairie: red dirt, old trees, harsh winters, hardy people, subtle hues, wide horizons, and unforgettable moons. He also sent poems about office politics, his grandmother's soft hands, his wife's love. Howard's poems had a practical and spiritual quality that appealed to me. Keen observations. Honesty. And so much grace and humility.

I started believing that God had sent a prophet just for me. I began posting his advices and admonitions in the *quiet place* of my soul. Howard warned me against thinking too much of high and mighty things and too little of all that is symbolized by the *featureless plain.* After all, the meek will inherit the earth. Like my students who will take my place, so will the bare plain, whether I learn to appreciate her beauty or not. *Prairie grass / Will grow again / From beneath / The steep snow drifts / Of our disdain. / Hearty straw, / Not we, / Will have / The final say.* Howard taught me that what goes on in mundane office affairs often rises to the level of a divine comedy or becomes metaphor for our deepest fears: death, isolation, loneliness, guilt. When Howard's computer malfunctions he worries that he is *incompatible with the network* and that *I could not save even to myself.* Howard taught me where to go to find God, love, and friendship. Abandon your armor of schedules and plans, he advises, and pay attention *To that no something / Or no someplace / In some anywhere / Of interstitial space / Where, unprepared, we meet / Face to face / Like Moses and his God.* We cannot orchestrate revelation or romance, we cannot say *I found you or / You found me.* We can only humbly say we had an *unexpected finding.* But if we are to have such findings, we need to be prepared for them by tending to our souls. Howard taught me to find a *quiet place / Where your face / Is not a mask* and *Where, though you're / Rent to pieces, / You're still whole.*

To put it plainly, Howard Stein's poems speak to my condition. Their language grabs my attention and their message lifts my spirit. It's not often one says this about poetry, but Howard's poems help me be a better person. From prairies to PowerPoint presentations to apple pies, no subject is too plain or too mundane, and every subject becomes a learning piece for life.

Preface

In October 1998, I gave a talk on aging, medicine, and literature at the Fifth Conference on Ethics and Aging in Tulsa, Oklahoma. I used much of my own poetry as the "substance" of the talk. Several days prior to the conference, Dr. Jeri Katherine Cooper, who would introduce me and moderate the entire meeting, telephoned me to obtain some information she would use in the introduction. She reminded me that we had met several years earlier at a health care ethics conference in Oklahoma, and that at least I was not entirely a stranger to her.

The morning of my talk, she presented me with a mysterious wrapped gift and a card. I was grateful but bewildered. *Why am I receiving a gift from her?* I wondered. A few minutes later, at my seat, I opened the soft package and read the card. In them, I found what soon became the title of this book. The quilted twelve-inch-by-twelve-inch cotton square, and the letter about it, went from "artifact" to metaphor. The gift of her "learning piece" felt uncanny: With it, I felt recognized, understood, even though her medium and mine were so different. I read from her letter at the beginning of my talk. What she wrote now finds its proper place at the beginning of this book of poetry:

> Last year, I took a class in hand quilting. I knew I would give my learning piece away but I was not sure to whom.
> After our conversation this week, I felt it had a home with you and those you love.

Traditional quilters tell of learning quilting from mentors. These mentors begin their students with a "learning piece;" that is, a square of material on which they would learn how to stitch. Once the students complete their learning piece, they start making the quilt itself and learn about the rest as they go. They "graduate," in other words. Veteran quilters, though, will say, *"Every quilt is a learning piece."*

So is every poem—and every book of poetry. It is something for which I hope eventually to find a home. If a poem begins as something of my own, I quickly wish to give it away to someone with whom it will be at home. Strictly speaking, even a poem which I author is not entirely my own. It comes from somewhere outside me. I become the home for the idea.

This collection of poems takes its title and image from the metaphor of quilt making and of learning to quilt. Although I do not make quilts, I make fabrics of ideas stitched with words—some poetry, some prose. I hope they will find a home in which they will be welcomed and understood. A quilter cannot ask for more; neither can a poet.

This book is a prairie quilt of sorts. Perhaps it is a collection of many quilts. It remains a learning piece. Everything finished is still preparation—even a completed book. In Dr. Cooper's words: "As long as it's fabric, it's possibility."

—Howard Stein
North Central Oklahoma, January 1999

Acknowledgments

I wish to acknowledge, with gratitude, permission to republish the following poems that were previously published.

"Prairie Paean," *manna* 12(1) Spring 1998: 2; "Weeds," *manna* 12(2) Summer 1998: 5; "Caulking the Wall," *manna* 12(3) Fall 1998: 4; "Rocking," *manna* 12(2) Summer 1998: 3; "Leaven," *manna* 12(4) Winter 1998–1999: 5. *manna* is a literary quarterly of manna forty, inc., Sharon, Oklahoma.

"Making Plans on the South Plains" and "Featureless Plain" *The Journal of Family Practice* 45(3) September 1997: 189; "No Haven," *The Journal of Family Practice*, 47(5) November 1998: 391; "Rash" and "Farm Couple," *The Journal of Family Practice* 47(5) November 1998: 392. Reprinted by permission of Appleton & Lange, Inc.

"A Moon for My Son," and "Keeper of the Watch," *Journal of Medical Humanities* 18(3)1997: 209, 210, respectively. Published by Plenum Publishing Corporation/Human Sciences Press, New York.

Reprinted with permission of Family Process, Inc., PO Box 23980, Rochester, NY 14692. "A Quiet Place" and "Thanksgiving," Howard F. Stein, *Families, Systems and Health* 1998, 16(3): 321. Reproduced by permission of the publisher via Copyright Clearance Center, Inc.

"My Center of the Earth," *AHEC News* (Northwest Oklahoma Area Health Education Center/Rural Health Projects, Enid, Oklahoma) October 6(1)1998: 2.

"Dad's Holy Drunk," *Fetishes, A Literary Journal of the University of Colorado Health Sciences Center*, Volume 5, 1999: 14.

"Likenesses" and "My Babushka" were originally published in *Sparrowgrass: Ten Years of Excellence* and *Treasured Poems of America*, 1999, by Sparrowgrass Poetry Forum, Sistersville, WV.

I wish also to acknowledge the unbridled encouragement of the following persons and organizations: Maxine Austin; Vivian Stewart; Florence Mason; Jeri Katherine Cooper, Ph.D.; Phil Floyd; Laura Ann Gall; Warren Holleman, Ph.D.; Paul Nutting, M.D.; J. Michael Pontious, M.D.; Valerie Gilchrist, M.D.; Elizabeth Ann Garrett, M.D.; John Frey, M.D.; Kathy Zoppi, Ph.D.; Richard Perry; Jackie Longacre; Mary Jac Rauh; L. Bryce Boyer, M.D.; Seth Allcorn, Ph.D.; Michael A. Diamond, Ph.D.; Rose Mersky, Ph.D.; Peter Petschauer, Ph.D.; Nance Cunningham; The Poetry Society of Oklahoma; the Don Blanding Poetry Society (northwest Oklahoma); and the Society of Teachers of Family Medicine.

A Quiet Place*

Have you found
A quiet place
No one can chase you
To or from?

Have you found
A quiet place
Where your face
Is not a mask?

Have you found
A quiet place
For your soul—
Where, though you're
Rent to pieces,
You're still whole?

* Composed for reading at receipt of Recognition Award,
The Society of Teachers of Family Medicine, Chicago,
Illinois, 24 April 1998.

Rising

I saw the sea
Rise up to shore,
But never thought
I'd see the time
When shore itself
Went out to meet
The sea—

Until the day
I heard your voice
And it rose up
Like firmest land
Into the gulf,
And reached across
To me.

Unexpected Finding

I found you or
You found me
Is too simple
A construction
For this unexpected
Finding.

I heard you then
I heard myself hearing;
I saw you then
I saw myself seeing;
You touched me then
I felt myself feeling.

I outstretched my arm,
Not knowing I was reaching for you
Until I reached you,
Then I knew
What an unexpected finding
You are.

Aunt Esther's Schnitzel

This, no battle for Novgorod
On the ice of Lake Chud,
No Stalingrad,
No Gettysburg,
No armada dashed at sea.
Only Uncle Jake
And Aunt Esther
Holding out one
Against the other
In the fort of time,
Inside the closed door
Of the toilet,
Stalling, waiting
For the other to explode.
"I need to go in," or
"When are you coming out?"
"Drop dead!" pierced
My effort not to hear.
"Why do we come here?"
I asked Ma—I was ready
To leave or disappear.
"The Schnitzel's worth
The shouting. No one
Cooks better than Aunt Esther."
Grateful for even
The smallest blessing,
I thanked God for the sound
Of flushing water.
The door would open—
Always from the inside,
Sullenness would stare
At sullenness;
The door would again close,
Sometimes pulled with a slam,

Sometimes with firm,
Silent triumph.
Then, thanks to God
For quiet,
Reprieve from these,
My people,
Jews at war.
You wouldn't think
Family would fight
Like that;
There are enemies enough.
Or maybe only family
Fights like that,
Battle enough
For any war.
"*Krank* and *Kadoches*,"
"Sickness and trouble"—
You wouldn't want to miss out
On Aunt Esther's Schnitzel.

My Babushka

Soft hands
Kind voice
Fresh bread

Grandmother's triad—
Or was it Trinity?
You brushed my hair
With a bow's long stroke
On cello strings.
You made your kitchen
A church dense with incense.

While I had you
I had no need for words
To parse a person by;
Your dying leaves me
Clutching for words
To keep you near.

Soft hands
Kind voice
Fresh bread.

Rocking

(For Zev Jacob)

My son at (a little over) three,
You climb and crawl
All over me,
Giggle and squirm,
Fashion some nest
Where you can let go the day,
Then nestle in and finally rest.

My son of (somewhat over) three,
You are my nighttime reverie.

A Moon for My Son

Lifeless world,
Who circumnavigates
My earth
And consumes
My attention,
I give you over
To my little son,
Who already at
Slightly later
Than one
Looks skyward
And exclaims
A gleeful, "Moon! Moon!"
At each sighting,
Or at each void
When I can only say,
"Soon, soon"—
A moon-absent sky
Is still enough;
Anticipation
And remembrance
Are a kind of
Fulfillment.

Billboards, Interstate East

Breakfast special, all you can eat,
T.G.I.5., Windsor Canadian,
You talk, we listen—bank with us,
Pepsi, Gotta have it,
K.O.O.L. all oldies,
The news leaders,
Why pay more?
Heart pavilion,
Hotel suite weekend rate,
Marlboro, Texaco,
Motel Six,
Easy rock,
Eight minutes ahead,
Exit here,
Exit now.

Winter tarries in the wind;
I still wear a heavy coat.
Yellow-green hovers
About roadside trees and bushes
With an aura not yet spring.
Daylight will soon bring
Sun and warmth.
I drive on,
Toward my office building,
Eight minutes ahead,
Exit here,
Exit now.

Business Meeting, Good Friday

Business meeting, Good Friday,
Around a thick oak table,
No veneer in this wood.
We met twelve to three
In the afternoon.
No sky blackened;
No earth shook.
We took note
Of more pressing business.

No Haven

There is no haven
From a prairie wind:
No tree
No barn
No house
No prayer—
A prairie wind
Will find us there.

Bullring at the Office

In this bullring, little ceremony,
Just business. No parades,
No fanfares, no picadors,
No toreadors—
Just men and women
In their business suits,
Standing around the coffee machine,
Seated at the conference table,
Riveted upon the PowerPoint presentation.

A bull among us is found,
At first like most of us
Standing or sitting around.
We tease. We taunt. We flirt.
We goad. We provoke.
We soon get what we want
From our prodding.
He charges. We move from his path.

He pulls away. We turn from him
And ignore him for a while.
We pick at him from afar,
With glances over our shoulders,
And with words in barbed whispers.
We flash our outrage in his direction.
He charges. After all, he is a bull.
What else can he do?

Still, we are chagrined
That he would attack us.
We are hurt by the thought.
What, we ask, have we
Done to him?

He pulls away. He snorts. He thrashes.
He charges at us again.
This time we draw our swords,
Plunge them into his flank,
Into his face, into his soft gut.
Blood arches in glorious fountains
All over the room, all over us.
It is warm and sticky on our suits.
We are pleased with our distressed carcass.

The ring is quiet. The ring will be quiet—
At least for a time, till another bull shows.

The bull—we tell ourselves—
Was a troublemaker, a loner,
Never got along, never accepted authority,
Never was really like one of us.
We are better off without him.
We turn away to go home,
To take these soiled clothes
To the laundry or the cleaners
Before the blood completely dries.

We turn back for one last look.
Shaking our heads,
We can only say,
"Bulls will be bulls."

Dispossessed

(For Zev Jacob)

As if I ever possessed you,
I no longer do:
A father's tenacity
A son's audacity—
And you are only four

But awesome
With a maestro's conviction
When I bid you listen
To the music on the radio:
"You listen to *your* Beethoven;
I'm listening to *my* Brahms!"
You proclaim with the ease
I associate with normal
Breathing, while you mark
The beat of yesterday's Brahms
That still has you in its hold.

You turn from me,
Lift your pencil-for-baton,
Then carry on
In complete disregard
Of over-worked loudspeakers
That run on mere electricity.

Evening Straw

Evening straw stands
Against the fading sky,
Against the railroad track.
Touch my winter husk—
Its ardor is not dead;
It will return in spring.

Sugar Donuts

My teeth crunch through sugar crystals
Into the moist dough of a morning donut.

I console myself with a second
As I reach for the grocery bag
My father brought home from shopping
In the Jewish district of town
Forty years ago.

Family Men, Family Stories

Men—even long-lived men—
Are a collection of marriages,
Impregnations, children, rages,
Drunks—lots of rages and drunks—
And funerals—lavish funerals.

Family sets fence posts;
The posts outlive the men,
Who are known mostly
By their cause of death
And place of burying.

Family reunions are
Temporary swarms
Back to the hive
Of those who remain.
All the in-gathered look around
And talk about those not there.

Women are the stuff
Of family lines;
They tend family
After men have
Disposed of themselves
Fussing, drinking, fighting,
Hanging, shooting, falling,
Despairing—mostly despairing.

Men learn at their funerals
Just how grateful their women
Were for them; women need
Their men, but they know
Men will amount to no good
No matter how long they last.
At church, the women
Now dressed in solemn black,
Pass the plate,
Collect their men,
And go on.

Family men
Have family stories:
Women, they
Are tree and forest.
Men are but
Strutting lumber.

Farm Couple

The fields are plowed and planted;
The wheat-husbander must rest and wait
Upon the furrowed ground
Who bears his seed—
Gestator, trickster, mate.

Featureless Plain

"Featureless plain"—
I've heard it again:
Nothing to see
But a disfigured tree
In a wandering creek-bed
Long run dry.

Too much bare land,
Too much bare sky.

Prairie grass
Will grow again
From beneath
The steep snow drifts
Of our disdain.
Hearty straw,
Not we,
Will have
The final say.

Feet First

I come here
In obedience to my feet,
Not thought through
Or told to go
In so many words,
No itinerary,
No map, no plan.

I only know
The going, the trek,
A head's blind trust
Of its feet—mine;
And should we arrive
At some destination,
It will be one
We both recognize
Unrehearsed—
Feet first.

Getting There from Here, or Remembering Ma's Pies

(Best read with a Yiddish lilt)

You can't get from here to there
Unless you take ground transportation
Or rent a car to get to the hotel,
The airport, the convention, the restaurant,
Or the shopping mall.
What did you think—
You could just go out
And walk there—

Like the way Ma
Used to make apple pies
By sending you down the street
To the grocery store for flour and spice,
Then told you to go up the hill
To the Conroys for apples
Right off the tree?

Everybody in the apartment house
Knew Ma was making pies
In her old gas stove.
I can still see her strudel crusts,
The way ground cakes in summer
Under the sun after a rain.
So crumbly those apples were,
I swear they grew in the oven.

I tell you, you can't get from here to there—
Without your own car
Or somebody to take you
And who has the time these days?
And when you get there
Where are you?

Out in the middle of nowhere
In your room or waiting for a plane.
Try to walk on those freeways
And you get killed.
Look. Go down the hall
And get some ice and a soda
From the machine.

If you listen to me,
You won't even try
To get there from here.

Halloween Mask

I remove my mask at Halloween,
As you probably do, though
Neither of us says so.
We say instead that we're putting one on.

For Halloween we assume
Costume, mask, and make-up,
Put aside the ordinary
"Real me" for all to see.

"It's just a mask," I tell you;
"My face is right behind."
The face, though, is
The mask of everyday—
As when I say "I'm not wearing
A mask, except on Halloween,"

Who am I fooling
With my trick-or-treat,
When, once a year, I unmask
The night the witches fly?

Never ask:
Which is face
And which is mask?

Imagine You

What do I do
When I can't imagine you?
I prepare for myself
A choice witches' brew
Assembled and stirred
In a single pot.
And when I'm through
I'll have cooked for myself
A most fabulous stew
Made entirely from ingredients
I'd imagined as you.

Caulking the Wall

I speak with you—
I attempt to speak—
You say you are listening;
You say you are speaking.

But all I see
Is a wall of brick.
You spend the time caulking
As we go on talking.

I keep walking
Into a wall;
You insist there is
No obstacle at all.

In the Space Between Desolations

In the space between desolations,
Do not give me words
And words again.

Give me silence
That fills a streambed
Till creeks could laugh.
Give me warm fingertips
And an open palm
That wrap a soft blanket
Aswirl with blood
Around my face and arm.
Give me breath
That carries sound
But touches first;
Give me what an eye can tell
And a word can say best later.

In the space between desolations,
Do not torment me
With unmusical
Virtuosity.
Do not beguile yourself
With shapes that have
No voice.

In the space between desolations,
Grant me the quiet of a leaf
Drifting downward,
Ripe with fall.

Intimation

You needed so few words
To shatter the glass
In which I thought
I had so well
Encased myself.

Could I have a wish
I didn't even know I knew—
But would recognize
When it was
Spoken by you?

"I love you dearly,"
You said—and I heard
From your lips
What I could bring myself
To say only nearly.

Keeper of the Watch

Death is not alone
The hour,
But, too, the timepiece
We reckon it by:
The sun, the clock,
The morning crowing
Of the cock.
Part of dying
Is the keeping
Of the watch.

Family Resemblance

If I must meet with you at all,
Permit me to confine it
To the conference room;
Please do not insist
That I have lunch with you also.
Business with your words
Across so vast an oaken slab
As this is already
Too close to lunch.
Coffee awakens me
To your tabulated deceits;
I replenish my cup often,
Lest I sleep in your slides
And budget projections.
I demur too often for your taste,
So you invite me to lunch
At the restaurant of my choice.
I work too much, take it all
Too seriously, you say—
So let's talk about it over lunch.
You are my superior;
How can I decline?
Though I do;
The poison in the patois
Is too much for any business lunch.
Shylock, I see you say
With your eyes;
I will admit
A family resemblance.
I have never taken
To merchandising lunch;
Think of it, if you can,
As a matter of principle.

Ancient Text

Broad arcs of pink and yellow
Stretch across the east
Before the sun.
The new sky shouts
An ancient text:
Where were you
When I reached my arm
Across the heaven
And brushed the earth?

Empty Cupboard

Give me the clutter
Of bowls and glasses,
The clatter of dishes.

No noisy reminiscences—
They only clutter
The empty cupboard
Of your dying.

Car Ride

(In memoriam, Paul Celan)

In the sanctuary of my motor vehicle,
He spoke with such diabolical candor
As to incline me to press toward
Our distant destination:

What is it with you Jews?
He began the unexpected trial.
You act just like the other Jews
I've known all my life,
Like you're all so special.
Look at Weimar before Hitler—
A turn in the road I should have
Expected he would take.
Jews were overrepresented
In government, in the arts,
In science, in medicine,
In the media, in everything.
They controlled the whole country.
Can't you understand why Germans
Wanted to get rid of them
To get their own country back?

I thought to pull over
And find a phone
To obtain for him another ride,
But I feared he would
Construe it as persecution.
I drove on, attentively—

You Jews bring persecutions
On yourselves; you Jews
Push your way into everything.
I know it's terrible to say—

And I'll deny that this conversation
Ever took place if you say anything
About it back at the office.
What happened to them
Was horrible, but much of it
Was of their own doing.
It's the same here in America.
Jews have infiltrated the government,
The arts, the news media, science.
They want to control everything.

And you're just like them.
You act as if everyone is against you,
And it's not true. You get surprised
When we push back. Your future
In the organization depends
On your ability to be less rigid
And to trust me. I'm looking out
For your best interests.

I'll say it again:
If one word about this
Gets out to anyone,
I'll completely deny it.
It is our secret, he said
With the slightest quaver.

We rode in silence
To our destination.
I felt endangered,
But must admit
To a minor thrill:
Outside the car,
He was as much
A captive as I.

My tormentor, my superior,
Your secret has no more power
Than mine. O great hunter,
You are now the hunted, too;
You are now a little
Of my own kind—a Jew.

La Mer, after Debussy

Play for me
No more dialogue
Of wind and wave.

Yours was the sea,
And the sea
Is no more.

Do not
Taunt me
With the shore.

Leavening

I found the bread
Made in Heaven.

The grain is God's;
You are the leaven.

Likenesses

The sky is like
The sea is like
The prairie and the plains.

Far gives way
To farther,
And farthest has no name.

Making Plans on the South Plains

"Talk to you later,"
Or "See y'all later,"
We say at each parting,
As if dread-tinged wish
Could be coerced into
A simple, declarative,
Understated, imperative.
"You'd better infer
The dread, 'cause
I'm not about
To say it outright,"
I think but don't speak.

What we don't say
Is between here and there
You or I could
Just as easily
Turn into road kill
As the next guy,
Armadillo, or skunk;
Or a silent MI
Or dissecting aortic aneurysm
Could wreck plans
Not to mention mess up
Unsuspected chests.

"But, but all means,
Don't linger at my door;
Be on your way,
You're late as it is;
And let me say again:
'Talk to you later,'
'See y'all later,'
And For Heaven's sakes:
Be careful!"

Meeting

We've got to
Stop meeting like this—
But we've never met.

We've met more
Like lovers
Than most
Lovers get.

Brackish Waters

I live in brackish waters
Where rivers meet the sea,
Where salty ocean swarms with silt
And makes a brine for me.

I am a creature of brackish waters
Where warm and cold collide,
Where nothing stays the same for long,
Where uplands greet the tide.

I would grieve my brackish waters
Were I confined to lake or stream—
To have no more those meeting places
Of wakefulness and dream.

Moonrise over Mesas, New Mexico

I have not seen
A moon so clear
As in this desert sky:
Lifeless rock rises
Over lifeless rock,
Moon above mesa.

Mute rocks speak, but not
In the tongue of the dead.
Sandstone reds chant
The evening prayers.

Trees take hold in crumbled
Rocks' despair of once-steep bluffs;
Sagebrush are their subjects.

This desert night is still
With truthfulness:
Unthinking rock
Does not hate.
A rising moon
Does not deceive.
Stone monuments
Do not promise
Eternity.

Night Driving

Shortly after dark
I drove through town.
The streetlights looked familiar,
But familiar was fifty years away,
And I was a passer-by.

Past the last house lights
Red taillights flickered ahead
Like steady candle flames.
They kept me company
With the stars.

Strange, to pluck reassurance
From receding car lights,
And familiarity from a town
I never knew.

It's the night that drives me
To such mistaken leaps.

No Telling

The prairie night
Smirks pink and rose;
It will not tell us
What it knows—

The secret of
Black sky that glows—
What most to dread,
Portents or snows.

My Center of the Earth *

My center of the earth
Has no angel's face.
It has spawned no special race,
Has no periphery beyond the reach
Of human grace.
It is neither more nor less
Than any other place.

It is instead,
Mostly flat and wide,
Fit for scrawny trees and wild grasses
Bred for defiance of extremes—
Like the sky vault
That can rise to heaven
And in the next hour
Crush with a thunderclap.

My center of the earth
Is where folk cede
The test of wills to God
And do not find it odd
Or embarrassing to do so.

My center of the earth
Is a mostly quiet folk
Who call little attention
To themselves,
Who measure honor by deeds,
Who give before they are asked.

My center of the earth
Is where the wind
Is as much a person as the sun—
Where, once the wind has ceased,
The holy stillness speaks
Of a heart that beats
At the center of the earth.

* Composed in honor of the tenth anniversary of Rural
Health Projects, Inc./Northwest Area Health Education
Center (NwAHEC), Enid, Oklahoma, November 1998.

Not Knowing

I do not know
What to do
With the mere
Thought of you.

November, December

November, December—
Oceans of din,
Spoilers of calm;
There are islands, though:
Hands gathered
Around the dinner table,
Prayer before uttered prayer.

November, December—
Praise the unsaid
Over the said;
Praise the living
And the dead.
Praise the snow
I cannot hear;
Praise the circuit
Of a year.

Office Space

You say: I take up too much space;
You mean: I occupy any space at all.
Where I am is where and who
You wish to be—to expand, to sprawl,
Into the office skin of me.

But you do not say so directly—
Only that I must move swiftly
To smaller quarters,
More remote quarters
Down the hall, down the stairs,
Down to the in-fact-anywheres.

"Couldn't he just take his things home?"
You asked in committee, not looking at me,
Then came later to offer private apology.

I move; you move me;
I keep out of your way.
I cannot keep out of your way.
I move further,
Never far enough.

Space is parable
For both our dying,
And you'd rather
I go first—
But you'll only say
We're out of space.

Old Timer

Wedding tree, hanging tree,
Witness, judge, protagonist
Of a prairie's more-than-century:
You were here for the land runs—
Before the land runs—
For the first winter wheat,
For the first barbed wire
To keep the cattle in.

Promontory, sentinel—
What stories could one
Old cottonwood tell,
Of lightning strikes
And audacity,
Of horizons like the sea?

Marrying tree, hanging tree,
Oh ancient one of the plains—
Tell us the secret
Of your tenacity.

On This Shore

(In Memory of Simcha Stein, 1992–1998)

We walk but for a time
On this shore.

It soothes our feet;
It swallows up
Our footprints.

It makes sand castles
Of empires and of dreams.

It washes conceits
Far out to sea.

The shore keeps us company
Until it must go on alone.

Organ Choice

Times and places compete
For certainty of where
Human essence lies,
Where, without it,
Something dies, if not us entirely:
Heart, liver, stomach, brain;
Gall bladder, pituitary, pancreas, spleen—
Some organ to be touched and seen.

Were I to chose a likely site,
I'd offer polite apology
To anatomy and physiology,
Then give chase
To that no something
Or no someplace
In some anywhere
Of interstitial space
Where, unprepared, we meet
Face to face
Like Moses and his God.

Recognition
Is essence's guise,
And all essence
Is surprise.

Overdressed

Don't chide me
For wearing
So heavy a coat.

What do you know
Of the bite
Winter air makes
Upon my cringing skin?

How could you hear
What I might say?—
How would I know
Where to begin?

Rash

Here, on the surface
Of my skin,
An attack from within.
"Histamine fire-storm,"
I called it in my half-science frenzy
To name the fury.

I replied to the assailant's
Relentless assault
With a counterattack of my own:
A leaf rake's-worth
Of fingernail scraping
Should have been enough
To numb any itch.

The scratcher, though,
Forgot the foe—
Until the rash raised redder
And itchier still,
As though to signal
To my unobservant eye
That we were—
Or at least should be—
On the same side.

Prairie Browns at High Winter

Prairie browns at high winter
Cast straw shadows long into dusk.

What luminescent dead!
What clever disguise!

I always knew this old rust
Had secret wealth set aside.

Preparation

Unwittingly we were wrong,
And for the longest time.

We thought we were bringing
You home from the hospital
Once and for all:
Each next time a cure,
Maybe from the medicines,
The doctors, the machines—
But you'd be back for good this time.

I don't know who made promises
Or who sought assurances,
But one day you surprised us all
By dying.

How clever you were
To rehearse us so well
In so unsuspecting a disguise:
How thoughtful a deception
To make a going seem
Almost like a return.

Progressively

(For Kenneth Bernard)

For the longest time,
They only told me
My computer was incompatible
With the network,
Later with the printer,
Then with e-mail,
Soon with my own
Floppy disk drive
When I could not
Save even to myself

Which was why
I felt isolated but was told
I wasn't, I shouldn't, how dare I,
Weren't they trying?
Until they gave me notice,
Without explanation,
Saying only that, "You are
In violation of the Law."

It was pointless for me
To inquire into particulars,
Since they were the Law.
When I pointed out
Their negligence and flaw,
They would only repeat
Their refrain: "You are
In violation of the Law."

When, for the last time,
I walked out the door,
I knew their equipment
Had finally been fixed.

Raining Buckets

"It rained buckets," my mother used to say,
Looking out our apartment window
After a thunderstorm.
I replied with downward eye,
Incredulous at such liberties
As she took with words.
I crouched beneath the piano
During lightning and thunder,
Expecting protection from an upright.
In the Ohio Valley, no deluge
Arrived in buckets;
Rain didn't even pour.

Oklahoma steppe-land, spring and summer:
When the sprawling red dirt is caked
Under a broiling sun, I wonder
How many eggs we could fry on this griddle.
When I look up into the sprawling vat
Of a horizonless sky
I'm sure some crazed painter with a surfeit
Pours pinks and blacks and grays
And grizzly violets
Into his play-bowl,
Stirs them violently into mighty vortexes
And delicate fans,
Lifts white creams to fifty thousand feet,
Then with a boisterous laugh
Dumps the whole thing
On the hot belly of the earth.
I watch this all
With a detective's eye for detail.
"It rained buckets,"
Is what I'd say.

Rainy Chicago

Camera in hand, loaded with film,
I came to Chicago to photograph buildings—
The Wrigley Building, stately,
Lit as a full moon;
The old apartment house on Greenleaf Avenue,
North of the Loop,
Where four decades ago
I visited my grandmother
And ate *borscht*
From half the neighbors' kitchens
In the building.
Voices carried
In canyons between windows,
Between apartment rooms;
Even the fire hydrants
Spoke loud Yiddish.

But the rains—unforecast—
Kept me away.
No wet lens will do
For majesty or for memory.
I sat in the hotel lobby;
I watched water course down
The huge window pane
In thick, parallel streams;
I watched the carefully appointed bushes
Bend dangerously low toward the lake.
I have no special gratitude
For the rain, except that
A corner outside
A hotel lobby
Gave me a Chicago
As well as could
Any dry lens
In the sun.

Reserves

Bales of hay,
Cut last spring—
They lean upon the house;
They lean upon the barn;
They lean upon the wire fence;
They'd lean upon the wintered weeds
If they could.

They are our provisions
Against a day
The snow sits too deep
For cows to graze through,
Or when the wind bites
Sharper than coyote-teeth.

Bales sit like military reserves:
They wait; they know
How bad it is when they are
Called up to serve.

Shards

(In Memory of Primo Levi)

In this place of desolation
I no longer fend off ancestral ghosts.
"Come. Join me at the table for a meal.
This place is still as much yours as mine."
There is no building without a gargoyle.

The chimneys of Auschwitz continue to spew.
Give me a garden-variety God
Who can collect all the ashes
And the decomposed bodies
In a single pool of tears.
What house is not made of ice
Kept under deep refrigeration?

How much blood-soaked ground
Beneath our still unformed massacres?
Unbearable increments
Break the backs
Even of the dead.

Beatific visions
Come in rings made from the glass
Of broken Coke bottles
And in discarded rims
Of pasta shells.

The new menu in the restaurant
Down the street reads:
    "We stuff
      Our taco shells
      With salads
      Made from private hells."
They tell me this selection
Already sells well.

In this place of desolation
I gain no merit from paying my bills.
The best hope is to be put
On a later train.
Deportation is destiny.

Even before the archaeologists come,
Shards are what we have made of this place.
There is nothing for them to dig
That we cannot gather for ourselves—
Tell them to stay home.

Simian Tree

I have swung
On the simian tree,
By branch and vine
Till all were mine:
The fleeing, the chasing,
The quick about-facing,
From low to high
On the simian tree.

I will no doubt fall
To some fatal bleeding,
But not before
I have given a heeding
To places made
Of rarefied air
And formative dust,
To heavens above
The farthest skies,
To spaces free
Of simian lies.

Slip of the Heart

A slip of the heart,
Blurted out from amid
The most well-groomed
Conversation.

What disruption
This *scherzo* makes
To my stately,
Daily *sarabande*!

To whom did I first
Reveal so composed
As heart as mine?
Did I surprise us both
With my undisguise?

My heart skips a beat.
The arms' length
I have kept myself
From you, becomes
The arms in which
I hold you now.

My cherished slip,
I clutch you as I would
A treasured gift.
You tell me the secret
Of my own heart.

Story Telling, or Flawed Narrative

I tell the wrong story;
I tell the wrong ending,
The wrong beginning,
The wrong middle,
The wrong moral,
The wrong point.

I tell the story in
The wrong rhythm,
The wrong cadence,
The wrong meter,
The wrong rhyme.

I give the story
The wrong hero,
The wrong villain,
The wrong fool,
The wrong substance,
The wrong form.

Whatever story I tell,
I keep getting it wrong.
Maybe there's no way
Of getting it right—
Or maybe all along,
It's supposed to be wrong.

Surfeit

Against a surfeit of words,
I strive to say less,
Even nothing.

I inquire
Of my expiration date.
A first quarter moon replies
That my inquiry
Serves no good purpose
But to batter the shore
With heavy froth.

A wave of sorrow
Washes over me.
I fall silent now.

There is so much
I do not need
To try to know—
Even less
To try to say.

Survivor's Wound

(In Memoriam, Paul Celan)

If none will see
    Atrocity,
Does the survivor
    Have a wound?

If I screamed
And no one
    Heard me,
Would I have screamed
    At all?

My torment is double:
    Holes in my flesh
    And holes in time.

I speak for the dying
    And for the dead:
Affirm, at least,
    My scream!

Nothing happened,
You whisper back—
    Nothing;
Your atrocity is
    But a dream.

If none will see
    Atrocity,
Does the survivor
    Have a wound?

Thanksgiving

You have never openly
Called me a turkey—
But you have given
Your share of hints.

You hollow me out,
Dispose of my insides,
Overstuff me to bursting,
Bake me to a golden brown,
Serve me at the table,
And call the occasion
Thanksgiving.

I sit and observe
Without saying a word.
What am I to think
Of so family an occasion?

The Chicken and the Wife*

My beloved, my wife,
My own Sabbath Queen,
Why do you twirl me
Around your shoulder
All these years of marriage,
Wring the neck
Of my soul
Like a chicken
At *Kapores* **
Just before *Yom Kippur*?

Sweetheart, mate,
My Jerusalem of gold,
Of copper, and of light,
Relent in your single-minded
Plan; tell me my sin
For which this fatal spin
Is punishment.

You, for whom the moon
Would bend her orbit,
Heed my petition
Before you snap my spine.
You, who are more sweetness
Than Sabbath wine,
Summon quickly the rabbi
Who wed us
So many years ago.
Let us ask him
If I am the right
Kapores for you.

Beloved, wait!
If you love me,
Do not mistake me
For a chicken!

* a poem in the manner of Gustav Mahler *Lieder*

** *Kapores* (pronounced kuh-póre-es) is an old, now fading, ritual practiced by many Orthodox Jews prior to *Yom Kippur*, the Day of Atonement. As an elder recites prayers of atonement, he holds a chicken securely (!) by the neck, and waves it three times over each penitent. It serves the purpose of the sacrificial scape-goat, except that it is instead a scape-chicken (scape-rooster, scape-hen).

The Ringmaster's Whip

The ringmaster holds steady
His whip before his lions.
They encircle him,
But he only stares
As he holds back has lash.

The tent is quiet.
No eye blinks;
Even the lions
Do not growl now.

No one sees
With what infinitesimal gesture
The ringmaster raises his whip
To pop the heavy air;
But the lions fly in a fit
Unbecoming to any circus tent,
And the night explodes in storm.

Dad's Holy Drunk

Dad promised he'd get drunk today,
And he did.

Today, twenty-one days after the New Year,
The earth completed another circuit of the sun.
In *Schul*, they read the last portion of the Torah,
The death of Moses, patriarch and lawgiver,
Liberator and herdsman of his unruly tribes.
After little more than a breath and a blessing
Came the Beginning once again,
When the Most Holy, Blessed Be He,
Called the world into being
And saw that it was good—
A good enough reason
To get drunk for the Sake of Heaven.

After the service, Dad went downstairs
To the social hall for cakes and sweet grape wine—and whiskey.
For all his more than eighty years,
He hobbled briskly to his drink.
The more the old men drank,
The more they began to sing—
In Hebrew, in Yiddish,
Once a year in sweet immoderation.
In good company, my dad drank
And produced all manner of
Signs and wonders in the land that day.

On *Simchas Torah*, the day of the Rejoicing of the Law,
Dad got plenty drunk.

Tides

To the beat of tides
The ocean surges
High upon the shore.
No sea can banish
Moon and sun
And be a sea no more.

Trunk and Branches

Night is still
In the trunk,
But golden light
Already dusts
The branches.

What am I to think
Of darkness?

Weeds

"Weeds"—best said
With snarl or sneer,
About these interlopers,
All of them queer,
Nameless, ugly, look-alike—

But stop! I discern
A distinctiveness here:
Black-eyed Susans,
Blue-stem, and
Tall prairie grass,
Blazing stars,
Purple clover—
Nothing crass
Or out of place,
No indiscriminate
Horde or race,
But a myriad
Of singularities,
Each with its own face.

No weeds,
But flowers instead
To unprejudiced eyes
Upon a prairie bed.

When the Feast Is Over

Sometimes, Thanksgiving feels like
A forced feeding—
The turkey, the company,
And the football game
That occupies the house
For the hours we force ourselves
To sit together in front of the TV.

I am most thankful
When the feast is over.
I can return to mere
Wafer and wine
For communion.

Without Windows*

(After Modeste Mussorgsky)

This place is without windows,
Without outside light,
Without outside air.
The seasons are changing,
But we would not know.

We work at our stations.
We imagine autumn.
We wear all varieties
Of religious amulets
To simulate the sun.

This place is all brick,
Dark glass, and metal.
It does not have windows;
It does not need windows.
There is nothing to see.

* Written for Fall Colloquium, 1998, Center for the Study
of Organizational Change, University of Missouri-
Columbia.

Words Come Last

My feet move
To a compelling pulse.
(I only later recognize
the rhythm as you.)
I dance—
(I can only dance.)
But do not know
I am dancing,
Until you tell me
I am dancing
With you.

Wotan's Voice Nearly Cracked

(Conclusion, Act III, Die Walküre, *Richard Wagner)*

Wotan's voice nearly cracked
As he placed his errant daughter
Upon the highest rock,
Cast a spell to make her sleep,
Then surrounded her with a ring of fire.

I don't know whether that radio voice
Was a man's or a god's
Or which is more in character—
To hold firm the melodic line
Or to burst into tears
For both man's and god's
Helplessness.

I have never heard such abject sadness
As from this Wotan
Whose song was cry
And whose cry was song,
As he sang to us
Of his brokenness,
And ours.

A Prairie Paean

My prairie, my kin,
Sagebrush-spined,
Tumbleweed-spiked,
You give me your breadth,
Your outstretched arm,
Your stillness, and your dread.
You give me your rough-hewn streams.

My prairie, my kin,
You are the skin upon my dreams.

Prairie Moonrise

While I was out for an early walk,
An unexpected eye-corner
Caught me by surprise:
A full moon-rise
Through cold-raked trees,
My prairie sky companion
Of a winter night.

In its long ascent,
The Scroll of the Law
Is what I saw
In blinding reflection
Of yesterday's sun.

Who are you, old stone friend?
Unnatural gift,
Inanimate world,
Unlikely sign
Of an unnamable God.

Dreaming

Dreams
I dreamed
I was dreamt

I was your dream
I have dreamt your dream
I have walked in your night

I am awakening now.